The Indians

The Indians

Pamela Odijk

M

The Indians

Contents

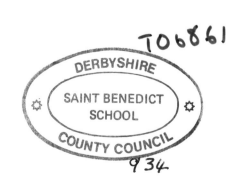

The Indians: timeline

Old Stone Age. The first people of India were the Dravidians. They lived in caves and other natural shelters, and were a hunting and gathering (nomadic) people.

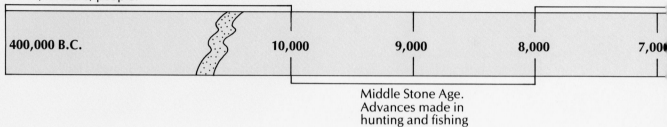

| 400,000 B.C. | | 10,000 | 9,000 | 8,000 | 7,000 |

Middle Stone Age. Advances made in hunting and fishing techniques.

The Vedic Age. The history, philosophy and religion of the early Aryan invaders was recorded in the *Vedas*.

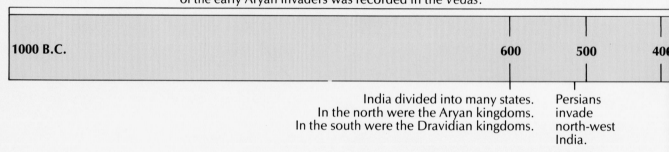

| 1000 B.C. | | 600 | 500 | 400 |

India divided into many states.
In the north were the Aryan kingdoms.
In the south were the Dravidian kingdoms.

Persians invade north-west India.

Rajput kingdoms.

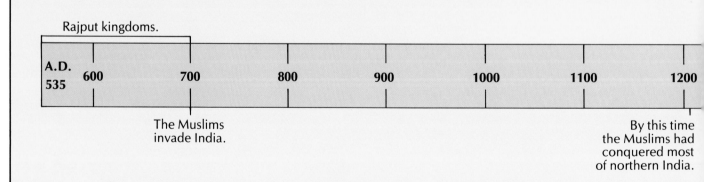

| A.D. 535 | 600 | 700 | 800 | 900 | 1000 | 1100 | 1200 |

The Muslims invade India.

By this time the Muslims had conquered most of northern India.

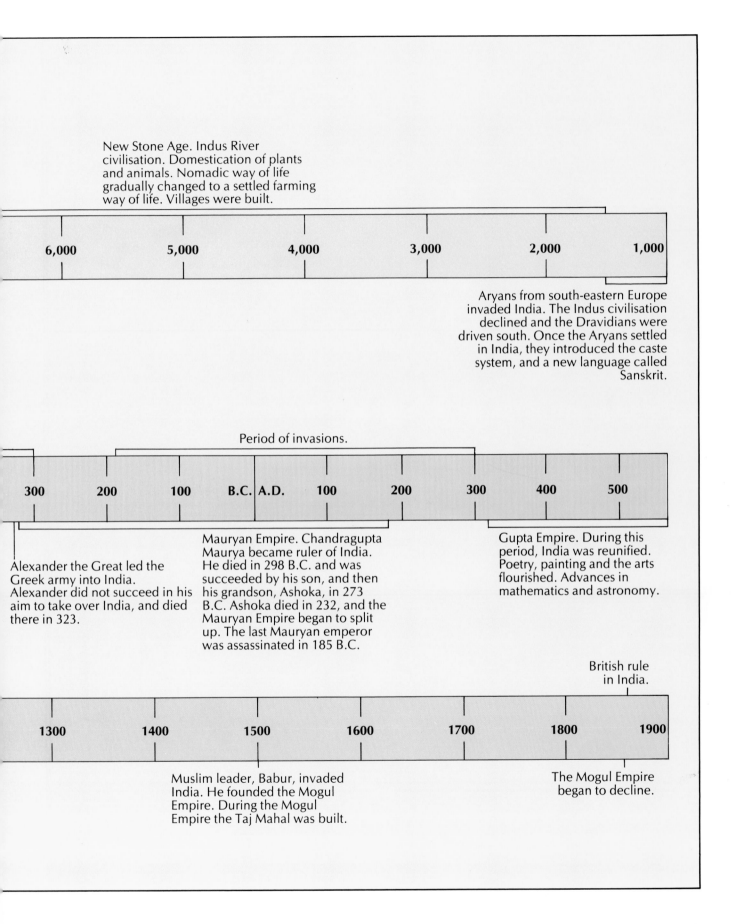

New Stone Age. Indus River civilisation. Domestication of plants and animals. Nomadic way of life gradually changed to a settled farming way of life. Villages were built.

6,000   5,000   4,000   3,000   2,000   1,000

Aryans from south-eastern Europe invaded India. The Indus civilisation declined and the Dravidians were driven south. Once the Aryans settled in India, they introduced the caste system, and a new language called Sanskrit.

Period of invasions.

300   200   100   B.C. A.D.   100   200   300   400   500

Alexander the Great led the Greek army into India. Alexander did not succeed in his aim to take over India, and died there in 323.

Mauryan Empire. Chandragupta Maurya became ruler of India. He died in 298 B.C. and was succeeded by his son, and then his grandson, Ashoka, in 273 B.C. Ashoka died in 232, and the Mauryan Empire began to split up. The last Mauryan emperor was assassinated in 185 B.C.

Gupta Empire. During this period, India was reunified. Poetry, painting and the arts flourished. Advances in mathematics and astronomy.

British rule in India.

1300   1400   1500   1600   1700   1800   1900

Muslim leader, Babur, invaded India. He founded the Mogul Empire. During the Mogul Empire the Taj Mahal was built.

The Mogul Empire began to decline.

7

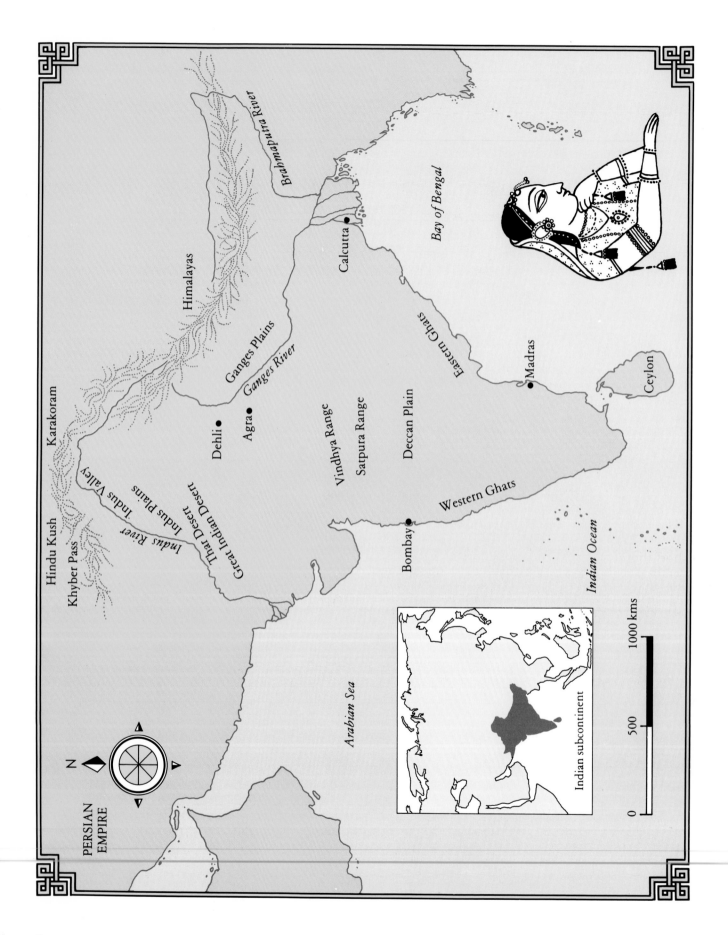

PERSIAN EMPIRE

N

Hindu Kush

Karakoram

Khyber Pass

Indus Valley

Indus River

Indus Plains

Great Indian Desert

Thar Desert

Himalayas

Dehli●

Agra●

Ganges Plains

Ganges River

Brahmaputra River

Calcutta●

Vindhya Range

Satpura Range

Deccan Plain

Eastern Ghats

Western Ghats

Bombay●

Madras●

Ceylon

Arabian Sea

Bay of Bengal

Indian Ocean

Indian subcontinent

0   500   1000 kms

8

The Indians: Introduction

The huge Indian subcontinent covers what is today India, Bangladesh and Pakistan, and has been inhabited since the early Stone Age. Along the Indus River Valley developed India's first civilisation, that of the Dravidians. The Dravidian people changed gradually from a nomadic people to a settled agricultural people.

As the Dravidians settled in villages, they established trade with other peoples. Gradually, their villages developed into towns and their culture flourished. From 1700–1500 B.C. the Indus Valley civilisation went into decline. **Archaeologists** are still trying to establish reasons for this decline.

From 1500–1000 B.C. the Aryan people who were nomadic herdsmen from south-eastern Europe made a series of invasions into India, and occupied the Indus River Valley. They moved toward the east, conquering lands, and established themselves in the Ganges Valley. The Dravidians who survived the Aryan conquest moved south and established themselves on the Deccan Plain.

By the 6th century B.C., India was divided into a number of kingdoms. In the north were Aryan kingdoms, and to the south were the smaller Dravidian kingdoms. The Aryans gradually spread throughout India, mingling with the non-Aryans, and from this came a common culture, and a common language and literature called Sanskrit.

The Aryan's religion eventually merged with that of the Dravidians, and grew together to form a new and more complex religion, Hinduism. The Buddhist religion became important in India during the 3rd century B.C. and remained important until the 7th century A.D. Eventually, some Buddhist practices were

Babur, founder of the Mogul Empire in the 16th century which ruled India for two centuries.

absorbed into other religions that became important in India.

In 322 B.C. the Mauryan Empire was established in India by Chandragupta Maurya. This was the first empire to unite all of India under one ruler. His grandson Ashoka became emperor in 273 B.C. He is remembered as being a great ruler. Ashoka became a Buddhist and had many Buddhist temples built. This empire eventually declined and a period of war followed until the rise of the Gupta Empire, (A.D. 320 to 535). The Gupta Empire has been called the Classic Age of India for during these years the culture reached its peak. Also during this time beautiful monuments were built all over India. The original Brahman (Hindu) religion gained popular support in the 8th century, by which time Buddhism had almost completely died out.

Chandragupta, founder of the Mauryan Empire, receiving his morning salute.

From the 11th century India was to undergo another change, when the Arabs, Turks, Afghans and Moguls came to India and brought with them another religion, that of Mohammed. Later, Christianity found its way to India with the Europeans. With the coming of the Europeans, Indian culture and civilisation was to undergo even further change. But by the time the British reached India the character and spirit of the old ways of India had already been changed and the old civilisation was finished. However, the West has much to learn from the old India with its tolerance, gentleness, greatness, understanding and achievements.

Time period	Some important events
to 2500 B.C.	Civilisation in the Indus Valley.
to 1500 B.C. (approx.)	Aryans invaded India entering through passes in the mountains.
500–200 B.C.	Alexander the Great reached India. Chandraupta Maurya founded the first Empire. He was succeeded by his grandson Ashoka who became a Buddhist and had many temples built.
A.D. 200–320	Period of invasions.
A.D. 320–535	Gupta Empire.
A.D. 535–700	The Rajput kingdoms rise.
A.D. 700	First Muslims rule India.
A.D. 1200	Muslims had conquered most of North India.
A.D. 1500–1850	Mogul Empire, founded by Babur.

The Importance of Landforms and Climate

The subcontinent of India is a triangular peninsula which covers an area of about 3 million square kilometres (1,158,000 square miles). It is separated from the rest of Asia by the world's highest mountains, the Himalayas in the north, tropical rainforest in the east, and desert in the west. The Indian Ocean borders the eastern Indian coast, and the Arabian Sea borders the western coast.

Throughout India's history the Himalayas have been important for many reasons. They have protected India from foreign invaders who could only reach India through a few narrow passages such as the Kyber Pass. The Himalayas are also the source of India's great rivers, the Indus and the Ganges. In the Himalayas also, are the world's highest snowfields and largest **glaciers**.

South of the Himalayas are the Ganges Plains which have been built up over the centuries by layers of **alluvial soil** deposited by the rivers. These northern Plains contain India's most fertile farmlands, which are regularly watered by the Indus and Ganges Rivers. It was on these Plains that India's earliest civilisations emerged. Further south a lower mountain range, the Vindhya Range, separates the southern plains, which are the Deccan Plains. These Plains, which are hot and dry for the most part of the year, were not as attractive to earlier settlers. The Vindhya Range hindered, but did not stop, the movement of people from the northern plains to the southern plains.

Jaiselmer Fortress town near the west Pakistan border (north-west India). The Jaiselmer castle (foreground) was built during the 12th century.

Mudumalai Sanctuary, southern India. The lush tropical rainforests in southern and eastern India provide a stark contrast to the northern and western deserts.

Climate

India has a tropical climate, that is mainly hot and dry. The Himalayas in the north stop the cold winds blowing across Siberia from affecting India. India's climate is dominated by the monsoon winds which bring rain. The **monsoons** have always been of great importance to India and rain is brought both by the south-west monsoon and the north-east monsoon. However, rainfall and temperatures vary over the huge distance and only a few centimetres (inches) of rain reaches far northern India and the south-east. India depends on the rain bearing winds especially in the south where there are no snow fed rivers to irrigate the crops or provide villages with water. The rivers are almost dry during the winter in this area. India receives 80 to 90 per cent of its annual rainfall during the monsoon season, and floods and droughts are frequent.

Natural Plants, Animals and Birds

Because of the variety of landforms in India, and the variations in rainfall and temperature, India supports a diversity of trees and plants, and animal and bird life.

In the west, along the coast and mountains, tropical rainforests are found where rosewood, ironwood, teak, bamboo and various softwoods grow. This gives way to **sal** forests, broad leaved forests, palms and tall grasses on the lower plains. Sandalwood and other trees providing fragrant woods grow in the south.

Along the foothills of the Himalayas many thousands of species of flowering plants and trees can be found including silver birch, fir, conifers, maple, large tracts of **mangroves** and both **evergreen** and **deciduous** forests. Elephants and rhinoceros roam the forests. Other animals found in India include bears, martens, weasels, otters, monkeys, **civet cats**, mongooses, wolves, jackals and deer. Wild buffaloes, **markhors**, **ibexes** and **yaks** have also made their homes in India and tigers are numerous. In ancient times, many of India's native animals and birds were sought by, and for, the Romans.

About two thousand different kinds of birds are native to India including vultures, falcons, hawks, parrots, kingfishers, herons, ducks, geese, peacocks and jungle fowls. Fish are plentiful in the rivers and lakes.

Among the species to be feared are **cobras**, **kraits**, **vipers**, and crocodiles. Mosquitoes and locusts have always been a problem for Indians.

Elephants have roamed the Indian landscape for thousands of years. The Indians had many uses for the elephant, especially during warfare, and as a means of transport.

Crops, Herds and Hunting

The earliest people to live in India were **nomadic** hunters and gatherers. They lived in caves and other natural shelters, and fed on small animals, roots and berries. During the Middle Stone Age (10,000–8,000 B.C.) they became more advanced in their hunting and fishing techniques.

By the New Stone Age from 8,000 B.C. onwards, further advances were made as these nomadic people gradually began to learn that certain grasses and crops could be planted, watered and harvested, and that certain animals could be domesticated and bred for milk, meat, wool and skins.

As these people began to cultivate crops and domesticate animals, they could give up their nomadic lifestyle for a settled agricultural lifestyle. Groups of people began to settle along the Indus River Valley.

From about 3,000 to 2,500 B.C., the Indus Valley civilisation began to take shape. Settled farmers established villages which gradually grew into towns. While some people continued farming, other people became established as craftspeople, making pottery objects for everyday use, as well as tools and implements from copper, bronze and stone.

The earliest farmers were nomadic farmers and used a "slash and burn" method of farming, which meant cutting down the trees and burning whatever lay on the ground. Once the growth was burnt, the soil was turned and then the crops were planted. The soil would lose its fertility after two or three croppings after which the farmer would move on and clear another area.

The settled people ploughed the land with a plough drawn by oxen or buffaloes. The Indian plough had no wheel and the part which cut the ground was a wedged shaped piece of hardwood. A pole in front was attached to the yoke of the buffalo or ox. Levellers or clod busters were used to smooth the surface of the field before sowing. Seed was sown in drills or by making small holes in the ground with a *dibbler* and planting a seed in each hole.

Crops such as rice, wheat, barley, peas, beans, lentils, spices and fruit (especially mangoes) were grown. Cotton and flax were also grown to make textiles. Dams, canals, artificial lakes and reservoirs were built as means of irrigation. The land was rented from the king by the peasants, and kings and princes had claim by way of taxes upon the people's crops. They could claim one sixth to one half of the crop as tax. Peasants' crops were also plundered and looted. However, the Greek travellers who came to India were impressed by the peasant farms and farming methods, and found it almost unbelievable that two crops a year could be grown. But if the monsoons failed there was no harvest and people had to seek food elsewhere. Famine and death by starvation were a part of India even in ancient times.

The yak found in the Himalayas and on the plateaus of northern India, were bred by the Indians for their wool.

Indian painting of Rajput nobles hunting. Hunting was regarded as a sport by the nobility. This painting also shows how elephants were used as a means of transport for the nobles.

Herds

The early Aryans were nomadic herdsmen. The Aryan word for "invasion" or "war" translated as "a desire for more cows". These Aryans raised cattle and used the cow without considering it sacred. Gradually these people became settled farmers.

Cattle were used for ploughing, transport and food products, and their manure was used as fertiliser for the fields, and as fuel. Often villages would employ a cowherd who would drive everyone's cattle to the grass beyond the fields each morning and return them at night. Each animal would be branded with the owner's brand. However, in the more remote parts of the country large herds were kept by professional herdsmen.

Goats were bred and in cooler districts, sheep were bred, too. The goats' wool fabric, kashmir, was widely used as was yaks' wool. Horses were bred in the northwest but were considered a luxury animal.

Hunting

Hunting was regarded as a sporting activity for the nobility. It was one of the Emperor Chandragupta's favourite pastimes and large hunting parties were organised. His grandson Emperor Ashoka became a Buddhist and put the ideals of Buddhism, which prohibited hunting, into practice. He gave up the hunt and forbade the killing of animals.

A half-wild pariah dog was common in early India, and dogs were used for hunting. In the hills a special breed of large dog was famous and sought after by other people as dogs of war and for hunting.

The hawk and cheetah remained wild in ancient India. Hawking and hunting with cheetahs was not popular with the ruling classes until the 11th century A.D.

Tame elephants were used from the time of Buddha. These had to be captured live as elephants rarely breed in captivity. Kings and chiefs were the owners of elephants and their forest reserves.

How Families Lived

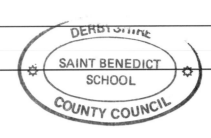

Extended Families

Indians lived in extended family groups. Children did not leave home when they married. Sons' wives would come to live in the house of their parents-in-law and would remain there and work as a servant of the house even if their husband died. In some places, a custom existed where the widow committed **suttee** (suicide) at her husband's funeral. Women had no rights or choices: they were expected to obey their father before marriage, their husband after marriage, and their father-in-law should their husband die.

Caste

Indian society was rigidly organised according to the **caste system** introduced by the Aryans, and each person's occupation was decided by the system. Everyone was born into a particular caste and their position in society remained the same throughout their life. Children were born into the same caste as their parents. It was considered unnecessary to do anything for a person lower down in the caste system.

The Indian caste system organised people into the following categories:

Houses

Indians built their houses using wood, reed or mud brick, and thatched straw. As most people were poor, they lived in small houses and had few possessions. Furniture was rare in India before the 16th century and even tables and chairs were seldom used. People sat, ate and slept on the floor. The interiors of the houses were very plain with only a small carpet or prayer mat to cover part of the floor.

Houses of the wealthy did not differ greatly from palaces. They were several storeys high; three-storeyed buildings were quite common. Early houses had vaulted roofs which were both thatched and tiled. In later times, roofs became flatter and had areas where people could sleep during the hottest times of the year. Houses had windows which overlooked the street, and walls were whitewashed and often decorated with painted pictures. Larger houses often had a square courtyard surrounded by a verandah.

Opposite: painting from the Mogul period which shows the construction of a palace. The division of labour in Indian society is shown quite clearly: the Vaisyas are directing construction, and those dressed scantily are the Sudras, the labouring people.

Brahmans	Priestly caste who were very powerful.	Pariahs or Outcasts	Unconverted native tribes, war captives and slaves. (In later times, the "untouchables" grew out of this group, and were considered the lowest people in society, and therefore "untouchable".)
Kshatriyas	Kings, nobles and great warriors.		
Vaisyas	Merchants, freemen including farmers and artisans.		
Sudras	Labouring people. Most people were in this caste.		

Ornamental trees such as the Chenar, an oriental plane tree, were favoured by the Indians for their gardens.

Indians were fond of flowers and trees, and wealthy citizens often had extensive gardens attached to their houses in which artificial pools and fountains were built. Favourite flowering trees were the asoka, with scarlet or orange blossoms, the sirisa, a tall tree with pale flowers, the kadamba, a fragrant orange flower and the kimsuka which was red. Bushes and creepers such as jasmin were grown. The most favourite flower of all was the lotus.

The peasant people in the country areas tilled their fields and grew crops. In the cities, craftspeople worked at various occupations including woodwork, ivory work, metalwork, bleaching, dyeing, soap making and glass blowing, as determined by their place in the caste system. Throughout the cities, and smaller towns and villages, roadways were used as bazaars and market places.

Women and Marriage

Marriage was compulsory in Hindu society and marriages were arranged by parents almost at the time of a child's birth. An unmarried man was considered an outcast. Girls were usually married at the age of twelve, but sometimes they were married at an earlier age and continued to live with their parents until they were twelve years old. Marriage was always between members of the same caste. In marriage, the man was master of his wife and his children, who were regarded as his slaves.

Generally a widow could not remarry but there is some evidence that remarriage was fairly common in very early times. The custom of sutte, the voluntary death of a widow on her husband's funeral **pyre** or soon after, was a common practice, but not throughout all of India.

Women's work was chiefly domestic work although women did take part in working the fields. According to Manu, a woman's main duties were to manage the house and attend to the family budget. According to the writings of the **Sutras** a man had to take his wife's advice on to how to spend his income and how to prepare the budget. A strict account of the budget was kept with her help.

Women born high up in the caste system were educated and knew the Sutras. In the early days of Buddhism, there was an order of nuns called the Sisters of Theri-Bhikkhunis.

Royal Families

Kingship was usually reserved for the male although a few families allowed a daughter to inherit the throne. Sometimes a queen acted as regent for her son until he was old enough to rule. Sometimes kings would nominate their successors which meant that the eldest son did not always inherit the throne.

The royal family lived in the court together with the harem of secondary wives and **concubines**. The Queen (*mahisi*) was all powerful and she often treated the other wives harshly.

Food and Medicine

Rice, **lentils**, vegetables and fruit were the main Indian foods. Meat, fish and fowl were only eaten by outcasts, though in earlier times, these foods were also eaten by the rich. After Buddhism became popular, contact with killed animals was regarded as polluting.

Most Indian foods were spiced with curry, ginger, cloves, and cinnamon. Other spices including the highly prized saffron grown in the Himalayan foothills. Chutneys made from vegetables and spices were served with meals, and the fruit of the **tamarind** was used to flavour curry. Rice cakes were cooked and steamed, and vegetables were often fried and served with fried breads and wafers. Dates were obtained from the area in the north-west, and almonds and walnuts were grown in the western Himalayas. Milk and curds were part of the Indian diet as was ghee (*ghrta*) made from melted butter by skimming off solid fat and leaving only butter-oil which would keep in a hot climate.

Food was served in bowls and eaten with the fingers. People usually sat on the ground to eat.

Food and Caste

The caste system had rules concerning food which had to be observed. The Brahmans only ate those foods which were prepared in the finest manner (*pakka*) while everyone else ate inferior (*kacca*) food. Pakka food was also offered to the gods at feasts. Also Brahmans would only accept cooked food and water from members of the same caste, and other people would accept food only from those whose caste was higher than their own. Feasting was done between people of the same caste.

Food which was left on a plate after a meal was regarded as *iutha* (scraps or garbage) and was considered polluted. Iutha could only be touched by someone of a lower caste than the person who had left the scraps. This food was either given to animals or people of lower castes.

Medicine

From the 6th century B.C. Hindu physicians could describe accurately many parts and functions of the human body. The greatest Hindu physicians were Sushruta, who lived during the 5th century A.D. and Charaka, who lived during the 2nd century A.D. Sushruta was a professor of medicine at the University of Benares who wrote a system of diagnosis and therapy in Sanskrit. This included surgery, obstetrics (the care of women before and after childbirth), diet, bathing, drugs, infant feeding, hygiene and medical education. Charaka composed an encyclopaedia of medicine which is still in use.

The Hindus were able to perform many surgical operations using 121 different surgical instruments. They were also able to perform skin grafts and limb amputations, and set fractures. They were aware of the importance of sterilising wounds and also of how to use drugs to dull pain.

Records show hospitals were being built in Sri Lanka (Ceylon) as early as 427 B.C. The sick were also taken to temples to be cured by **hypnosis** or temple sleep (sleeping in the holy place).

The Indians' doctrine of non-violence and respect for all life forms included animal life. Animal refuges and homes for sick and aged animals were set up. Horse and elephant doctors were skilled and respected professionals who became even more important in later times.

Clothes

In India's warm climate, clothing was not worn as a means of keeping warm. Beggars usually wore no clothing at all and until the time of the Muslim invasions it was customary for men and women to go about naked above the waist. The only clothing worn by children were ornamental beads and rings. Clothing worn in early times consisted of draped garments.

Men

Men usually wore a **dhoti** (originally called a *paridhana*) which was a loin cloth. In very early times it was worn by both men and women but later came to be a man's garment. It was made from lightweight cotton and was worn wrapped around the hips with one end being brought up between the legs and tucked into the waistband so it resembled a pair of baggy trousers.

Women

The main garments for women were the **sari** and the **khaddar**. The sari was a very long piece of colourful and often embroidered silk or cotton which was wrapped around the body, tucked and draped, with one end left hanging over the shoulder which could be draped over the head. The khaddar was a piece of hand-spun coarse cloth which was worn over the shoulders and clasped at the waist with a cloth girdle. This garment was long, reaching down to the feet. Shoes were seldom worn, but those that were, were usually made of cloth.

This 18th century painting of women throwing coloured powders during the spring festival of Holi, is a good indication of the style of clothing worn by women during this time.

Hair

Hair was usually oiled as protection against the drying sun. Men parted their hair in the middle and it was drawn together in a tuft behind the left ear. Although early sculptures show men wearing large turbans, they were not common until after the Muslim invasions during the 7th and 8th centuries.

Women wore their hair hanging loose except for one coil. Women decorated their hair with flowers and scarves.

Jewellery

Jewellery was worn by both sexes and although men's jewellery was confined to bracelets, women wore bracelets, anklets and rings. A ring in a woman's left nostril indicated that she was married. A symbol of religious faith was usually worn painted on the forehead.

Cosmetics

Cosmetics were used by both sexes. A common cosmetic was a paste made from the finely ground dust of sandalwood which was smeared over the whole body in patterns. It was sometimes coloured with **lac** and other dyes. Apart from its cosmetic use, it was also cooling on the skin.

An eye shadow (*aniana*) was made from black powdered antimony, which was a metallic element, and worn to enhance the eye and it was also thought to prevent eye diseases.

Vermilion (*sinaura*), lac (*laksa*) and a yellow pigment called gorocana were used to paint a spot on the forehead (*tilaka*). Lac was also used to colour fingers, toes, palms and the soles of the feet.

Jewellery was popular and worn by both men and women. This gold torque was worn as a necklace by women.

Fashions

Although most Indian garments were unsewn, the art of sewing was known as some fashion trends show. During some periods, Indian women are shown wearing jackets or bodices, and during the Gupta empire (A.D. 320–535) men wore trousers. On the coins of the time, Gupta kings are often depicted wearing trousers. Some kings are shown wearing long quilted coats and trousers as well as Asian style boots which must have been very uncomfortable in India's hot climate.

Royalty and Emperors

The royal processions, especially those of Chandragupta, were splendid occasions but the contrast between rich and poor was very evident. Accounts have been written of the emperor being clothed in fine muslin robes embroidered with purple and gold, and being carried in a gold **litter** decorated with pearls. He was accompanied by his guards mounted on elephants emblazoned with gold and silver. Some of the procession carried trees in which live birds were perched, while a flock of trained parrots hovered overhead.

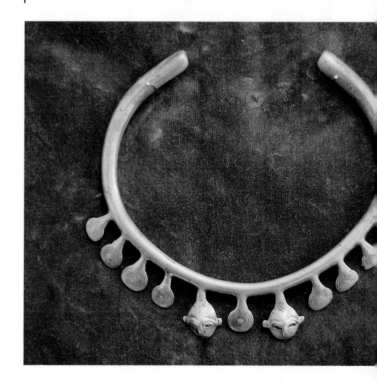

Religion and Rituals of the Indians

The oldest religion of India which the invading Aryans found was the worshipping of nature. Our knowledge of the Vedic gods comes from the **Vedas**, a collection of hymns completed by Aryan scholars in about 800 B.C.

The Hindu Religion

Hinduism was built into the Indian caste system where the Brahmans were the all important caste as well as the keepers, recorders and transmitters of knowledge. There were many ceremonies and rights which belonged to the different castes of Hindus and these are set out in the sacred literature. Sudras were not permitted to hear readings from the sacred books.

From 800 B.C. onwards, Hinduism changed and became less concerned with hymns and sacred books, and more concerned with complicated rules and philosophies such as how to discover and describe the inner truths and meanings of life or the search for enlightenment.

Left: stone sculpture of the Vedic god, Varuna, from the 11th century.

Some Vedic Gods and Goddesses	
Varuna	Prime mover and creator of the universe who punishes those who transgress the laws.
Indra	King of three worlds; storm god and wielder of thunderbolts.
Vayu	God of air or wind.
Agni	Fire god.
Chandra	God of the moon and fertility.
Surya	Chief sun god.
Ushas	The dawn.
Ratri	The night.
Vishnu	God of the sun's energy.
Sarasvati	Water goddess.

Some Hindu Beliefs

> **Reincarnation** The belief that the souls of all pass from one life to another.
> **Karma** The belief that good deeds were rewarded in another life and evil acts brought sorrow.
> **Several Heavens** In which there were separate gods.
> **Samadhi** The belief of inner peace which all could reach with effort.

Hindu worship was demonstrated in many ways, such as worshipping domestic gods at small household shrines near the kitchen, taking offerings and flowers to the local temple, and going on distant pilgrimages. Almost every aspect of life had a religious rite including everyday acts such as washing and dressing.

Sacred Cows

The cow was, and still is, the most sacred of all animals to the Hindus. Images of cows and bulls adorn the temples, and the animals themselves were free to roam the streets and countryside. Under no circumstances were these animals to be eaten or any products made from their hides worn. Cow manure was used in holy ointments and as fuel. When a cow died, it was often given a ceremonial burial.

The Ganges River was, and still is, sacred to the Hindus. It is believed that bathing in its waters washes away all sins. The tributaries of the Ganges are also considered sacred.

Some Hindu Gods and Goddesses

The Hindu religion has many gods and goddesses, and some are more popular than others.

Brahma	The creator, thought to be the greatest of gods because he set the universe in motion.
Shiva	The destroyer, who represents power; also the demon slayer. Usually depicted with several arms.
Vishnu	The preserver. To many Hindus he is the universal god, and is usually depicted holding four symbols: a discus, a conch shell, a mace and a lotus.
Paravati or Mahadevi	Shiva's wife. She represents the unity of god and goddess (of man and woman).
Matsya	The horned fish, who warned Manu (the first man) at the time of the mythological great flood and saved him.
Kurma	The tortoise who appeared on earth after the flood to retreive treasures.
Krishna	The hero god.
Buddha	An incarnation of Vishnu. Hindus believe Buddha came to teach the world to have compassion for animals.
Garuda	King of the birds.

Buddhism

There are some similarities between Buddhism and Hinduism as they both evolved from Indian thought. The Buddhist religion was founded by Buddha (or Siddhartha, 563−483 B.C.) Gautama who was born of a wealthy northern family. In his early years, having seen many distressing things, he decided to live poorly until he discovered the inner meaning of life. He then became Buddha, the Enlightened, and set about teaching what he knew. He called his teaching the "Middle Way".

To a Buddhist, enlightenment could be reached by following the eightfold path and four noble truths.

The eightfold path

Right views	Right livelihood
Right resolve	Right effort
Right speech	Right recollection
Right conduct	Right meditation

The four noble truths

The truth of sorrow (man is doomed to sorrow).

The arising of sorrow (because of striving for individual fulfilment. One should seek identity with other things).

The stopping of sorrow (or the craving for individuality must be overcome).

The way to stop sorrow (by following the eightfold path).

Buddhism changed over time, and Buddhist practices varied from one part of India to another.

Jainism

Jainism was also an important religion in India, and began during the 6th century B.C. Jains followed the teachings of Jina, or Conqueror, *Mahāvira*. There were many similarities between Jainism and Buddhism and although Buddhism spread to other lands, Jainism always remained in India. This religion also questioned the **Vedas**, opposed the sacrifice of animals, disapproved of the inequality of castes and preached non-violence. All Jains were **vegetarians**, and even the accidental killing of animals and insects was to be regretted.

Jainists believed the universe to be eternal and divided it into a number of cycles with a period of improvement always following a period of decline. Jainists also believed that everything including people, animals, trees and rocks had a soul and that karma surrounded the soul. The karma depended on the nature of activity around the soul. They believed that the soul constantly attempted to free itself to reach the top of the universe where it would remain blissful forever.

Hindu Wedding Ceremony

The bridegroom, dressed in his wedding clothes, would proceed to the bride's house in the company of friends and relatives. Here he was received by the bride's father and offered a *madhuparka*, a ceremonial drink of honey and curds.

The ceremony itself was held in a brightly decorated pavillion. The bride and groom would arrive separately at the pavillion and sit either side of a curtain. As sacred verses were chanted by the brahman, the curtain was removed enabling the bride and groom to see each other, often for the first time. The bride would be offered to the groom by her father and the groom would promise to care for her.

Offerings of ghee and rice were made on a ceremonial fire with the groom leading the bride by the hand around the fire. The bridal garments were knotted together. The bride then trod on a millstone after which the couple took seven steps together, treading on a small heap of rice with each step. The ceremony concluded with the couple being sprinkled with holy water.

Obeying the Law

The laws of early India were built into the caste system, and as such, were also a part of Hindu beliefs. Family groups ensured that each of its members behaved according to the rules of caste and religion as the misbehaviour of one member would bring criticism (and perhaps punishment) on the whole group. All groups had set rules which included rules of marriage, eating, learning and other behaviour. The penalty for breaking a rule was first to be expelled from the group. In some cases specific punishments were laid down.

Most laws were not written down, but were a part of social and religious behaviour. There was comparatively little crime in Hindu society. One of the most powerful of these unwritten laws was the law of karma, by which it was believed a person would be rewarded or punished in the next life depending on the deeds done in the present life. The other powerful law was the rule of **dharma**, which was to accept one's place in the caste system without question and to observe all the rules of one's caste.

Code of Manu

Manu-smrti or the "tradition of Manu" was the name given to the book of the Hindu code. It is attributed to Manu, the first lawgiver and dates back to the 1st century B.C. It describes what is expected of a Hindu as a member of each of the four social classes throughout his or her life. There was no difference between religious law and secular (non-religious) law.

Laws of Property

The code of Manu stated that wives, sons and slaves were not to hold property, and any property that they might earn was automatically the property of the master of the household.

Justice

Courts varied from place to place but a bench of appointed magistrates was more common than a single judge. There were complications concerning evidence as only certain witnesses were considered qualified. Others such as women, learned brahmans, debtors, persons with previous criminal records and persons with physical defects were not allowed to give evidence. Also, low caste people giving evidence against high caste people was not valid.

Ordeal (by fire and immersion) was often used to obtain verdicts. One unusual ordeal required the accused to touch a red hot ploughshare with his tonque.

Babur, founder of the Mogul dynasty in the 16th century, receiving advise from his officials.

Writing it Down: Recording Things

The earliest found records of India from the ancient Indus civilisation, are archaeological ones. Buildings, utensils, tools, inscribed seals, carvings and the oldest coins in the world have been found. A seal composed of two serpents' heads was the characteristic symbol of the Dravidians. These ancient people had a written script which, as yet, cannot be deciphered.

The *Ashokan Inscriptions*, which are engraved scripts, are the earliest important written Indian documents. There are two scripts: the *Brāhmī*, which was read from left to right (the origin of which is uncertain), and the *Kharosthī* (which was derived from the Arabic alphabet used in Persia). Scripts were also developed in central India and the Tamils of the south evolved their own regular script called *Grantha*.

With the development of the caste system the Brahmans came to be the recorders and transmitters of knowledge. Originally they relied on **oral transmission** of their laws, customs and myths, and the Brahmans made themselves powerful by emphasising their own importance.

From the 5th century B.C. the standardisation of languages began and India came to have a commonly understood language, **Sanskrit**, which was originally an Aryan language used in ceremonies. The work sanskrit means "prepared, pure, perfect and sacred". During the Vedic age when the Aryans settled in India, there was not one language but many as each tribe had its own dialect.

Sanskrit came to be the language in which sacred literature and folklore were written. There developed two types of sanskrit: the Vedic sanskrit, the language of the Vedas in which the hymns and chants of the Aryans were recorded; and classical sanskrit, which was the standard language of later times. Other languages such as Prakrit, Hindi and Bengali were also used. Pali was a particular form of Prakit, and became one of the sacred languages of Buddhism. Other written languages were Tamil, Kannada, Teluguana and Malayalam. India has never had one language.

Writing Materials

Books in ancient India were made by binding together a number of handwritten scripts. Scripts were written on the leaves and bark of the palmyra and talipot palms. These were dried and smoothed, cut into strips and joined together at the top and bottom, and then folded like a screen or concertina, or they were joined together by cords threaded through holes and held in place by two long narrow boards. The bark of a birch tree was sometimes used, too. Other materials on which scripts were written included cotton and silk, and thin strips of

Brahman expounding the Veda. *Much of the history, philosophy and religion of the early Aryan conquerors was expressed in a body of literature known as the Veda.*

wood and bamboo. Ink was made from **lampblack** or charcoal, and writing was done with a reed pen. In southern India letters were scratched on the surface with a stylus. Ink was then rubbed over the surface, and then wiped so that the ink only remained in the scratches. Paper is usually thought of as being invented in China but it may also have been known in northern India.

Calendar

The Hindus divided the skies into constellations of the zodiac and devised a calendar of twelve months of 30 days each, and added an intercalary month every five years. The basic unit was not a solar day but a *tithi*, which was a lunar day. Approximately 30 *tithi*, made up a lunar month, which equalled four phases of the moon. Each month was divided into halves (*paksa*), one beginning with the full moon (*pūrnimāvāsya*), and the other half beginning with new moon (*amāvesyā* or *bahulāvsyā*). A group of two months made up a season (*rtu*).

> *The six seasons*
> Vasanta (Spring: March-May)
> Grīsma (Summer: May-July)
> Varsā (The Rains: July-September)
> Śarad (Autumn: September-November)
> Hemanta (Winter: November-January)
> Śiśira (the Cool Season: January-March)

The solar calendar was adopted in later times, although it was known of during Gupta times.

Other astronomical calculations made by the Indians included the diameter of the moon, eclipses, the position of the poles and the position of the stars. In order to make these calculations, the Indians invented a system of mathematics superior (except for geometry) to that of the Greeks. Arabic numerals and the decimal system originated in India, reaching the West by way of the Arabs.

Painting from the Mogul period of an Indian astrologer using an an astrolabe and zodiac tables to make astrological calculations.

Indian Legends and Literature

India's oldest literature is the Vedic literature, which is religious literature. It was originally passed on by word of mouth and later written down in Vedic sanskrit.

Each Veda has four sections: the *Mantras* (Hymns), the *Brahmanas* (manuals of ritual, prayer and incantation) for priests, the *Aranyaka* ("forest-texts") for hermit saints, and the *Upanishads* (confidential conferences) for philosophers. To these are added the *Sutras* which are texts of explanation. The word Veda means knowledge and these books of knowledge were regarded by the Hindus in much the same way as Christians regard the Bible.

The Epics

There are three great epics upon which Hinduism is based. They were written down during the Golden Age of the Gupta empire, in the Sanskrit language. A description of each epic follows in the table below.

This 18th century Hindu painting shows Krishna playing his flute under the sacred Kadamba tree.

The Ramāyāna	This is the story of Prince Rama who went to Ceylon (Sri-Lanka) with the help of the monkey god Hanuman to regain his abducted wife Sita from the demon Rawana (or Ravana). It recounts the battles fought, and is a story of brotherly love and wifely devotion, and of good conquering evil.
The Mahābhārata	This is the story of the war for the throne between the Pandava kings and their cousins the Kaurava. It is a story about people's place in the universe and what causes things to happen.
The Bhagavad Gita	(Song of the Lord). This is part of the Mahabharata and is the story of Arjuna, the hero of the Pandavas who doubts the purpose of war just before he is to fight in battle. The god Krishna, who is disguised, points out that it is his duty to fight a righteous war. Krishna then reveals other things, such as the path to God and the nature of the universe.

Panchatantra (or Pañca-tantra)

This is a collection of Indian animal fables, many of which were translated for the Persian kings in the 6th century A.D. Later a copy was translated into Arabic. The popularity of the fables grew and more translations were made into Turkish, Greek, Hebrew, German, Spanish and Latin. In the Middle Ages many writers drew their inspiration from these Indian fables, including La Fontaine and Hans Christian Andersen. *Hitopadesha ("Good Advice")* is a selection and adaption of tales from the *Panchatantra*.

Many Hindu tales are also found in *A Thousand and One Nights* but these have been fused with Arabian stories and retold many times. Other collections of tales include: the *Vetāla-pañcavimśa-tikā (Twenty-five Tales of a Ghost)*, the *Sūkasaptati (The Seventy Stories of a Parrot)*, and the *Simhāsana-dvātrim-sātikā (Thirty-Two Stories of a Royal Throne)*.

Sanskrit was not the only language used to record Indian literature, and there has been a great deal of literature written in the Tamil, language. Although the earliest Tamil literature was not concerned with religion, it began to be featured more prominently from the 7th century A.D.

This 17th century Hindu painting from the epic tale Ramayana, shows Prince Rama's marriage procession.

Art and Architecture

Painting, sculpture and architecture were not regarded as separate crafts in early India, and a single craftsman might have combined all of these skills. In later times, these areas became specialised. Much Indian sculpture, painting and architecture were deliberately destroyed by the Portuguese and by the Muslims who not only thought Indian art obscene but wished to replace Indian religious art with their own.

Painting

Very few early Indian paintings have survived. The best surviving examples are the masterpieces at the temple of Ajanta which were dug out of the steep rock face. After the Muslim invasions Indian painters turned to painting miniatures and to illustrating books. Miniature painting was known before the Muslim invasions but only a few examples have survived.

This miniature painting of the Hindu god Vishnu riding on the back of garuda is from the 18th century.

Sculpture

Sculpture from earlier times is prominent in India, with temples bearing many relief carvings and statues. Most sculpture is in the form of carved human figures representing Hindu gods and goddesses (particularly Vishnu, Ganesh and Hanuman), mythical beings and fantastic animals.

Early Buddhism did not approve of statues but the school of Buddhism called Mahayana Buddhism was more tolerant and allowed many statues of Buddha and bodhisattvas. Some statues of Buddha were carved so that light shined on the Buddha from different directions, showing different facial expressions. Some of the most exceptional and beautiful sculptures are at Sānchī.

These elephants were carved, in relief, on the walls of a temple in southern India. This picture shows a segment of the wall, and is a fine example of the excellence achieved by those who practised this art.

Metalwork

Objects made of copper and bronze were common in India as porcelain and china were not in general use. Indian bell-shaped vases with long necks, which were used for carrying and storing water, show the excellence of Indian craftsmanship. Brass was shaped into a variety of bowls and containers and a black alloy of zinc was often used with one metal often being inlaid or overlaid with the other.

Metal images of gods and goddesses were made for worship. Nearly all Indian bronzes were made by the "cire perdu" method, where the design was first made in wax and then covered by a coating of clay. This was heated to melt away the wax, and then molten metal was poured into the mould. Very large figures were made in two parts and welded together.

Ivory Carvings

Very few ivory works have survived. One of the most beautiful examples is a statuette of a goddess found at Herculaneum which is thought to have been imported from India.

Architecture

As early Indian buildings were built using wood, they have long disappeared. The first stone buildings date back to Ashoka's time.

Stupas (or **topes**) were among the earliest monuments and were constructed by the Buddhists. These vary in size but have the same dome shape surrounded by stone railings with a monument on top. The great stupa at Sanchi dates from about 250 B.C. A few Indian stupas exceed the size of the one at Sanchi and those of Sri Lanka (Ceylon) were enormous. In northern India, stupas were very tall structures. Stupas were very ornate structures. The panels of the stupa of Amaravati illustrate the life of Buddha.

Buddhist monasteries are examples of early architecture. The walls of these were very thick and withstood the Muslim attempts to destroy them.

During the years of the Gupta empire, Indian temples came to be built above the ground. There were thousands of shrines built, each dedicated to a particular god. The largest number was at Bhuvaneshvar where 700 temples were built along the shores of a sacred lake.

Man Singh Palace in Gwalior, a city south of New Delhi in northern India. This palace was built in about 1560. The main gate and east wall are shown here.

The heart of the temple contained a shrine room (*garbhagrha*) with a hall for worshippers (*mandapa*) leading off this. The hall was sometimes a separate building joined to the shrine room by a vestibule. A porch (*ardhamandapa*) was at the entrance to the hall. The shrine room often had its own tower. Smaller additional shrines were sometimes also built. Each temple had its own courtyard and gateway.

Temples often operated as cities within themselves having many employees such as priests, musicians, attendants, dancers, scribes, craftsmen and labourers. They often had schools and refuges for sick people and animals, and it was to the temples the population came in times of distress and famine.

Jain Temples

In the 11th and 12th centuries the Jain temples were India's finest. At first these resembled the Buddhist style but acquired a style of their own. The Jain shrines contained many statues of Jain heroes. High above the desert on Mt Abu are two surviving temples, Vimala and Tejahpala, which are considered to be the greatest of the Jain artistic achievements. The temple at Vimala was built entirely of white marble.

Palaces

Cities had two central places: the palace and the temple. However we know very little about the palaces of old India as only fragments of these buildings remain. It is thought that palaces were built in or near the centre of cities.

Going Places: Transportation, Exploration and Communication

Road Transport

Transport for ordinary people was either on foot or by two-wheeled animal drawn carts. The nobility and royalty were borne by litter or carried on the backs of elephants. Roads were constructed over which horse drawn chariots could move quickly. However, the Indians did not master bridge building; instead they used ferries to cross the large rivers. In times of the monsoons, travel in India virtually ceased.

River Transport

The great rivers, especially the Ganges were used to transport goods and people. The Indus and other rivers of the Deccan Plains were also used as trade routes.

Trade

India in ancient times was one of the richest countries in the world and traded with Europe, the middle-east and Asia. Ships carried cargoes of textiles, gold, spices, perfumes, dyes, Indian silks, Indian ivory and animals such as cheetahs, tigers and elephants for the bloody gladiatorial combats in Rome. The chief ports of India were Bhrgukaccha on the west coast, Supāra near Bombay and Patala on the Indus Delta.

Although India has always had a sea trade, the people treated sea travel with a certain fearfulness. After the Muslim conquest, travel to foreign lands incurred penalties.

18th century painting of Raja Balwant Singh hunting partridges. The Raja is being transported in a litter, borne by his servants.

Music, Dancing and Recreation

Indian music has a long history of at least three thousand years. The Vedic hymns were written to be sung, and poetry, music and dance were all part of Indian ritual.

Indian music had a peculiar quality and a sound of its own mainly because it is written in a scale of twenty-two quarter tones which is very different from the scale of twelve tones of Western music. There is no harmony in Indian music, only melody. A musician would select a theme or *raga* of five or six notes which was repeated frequently throughout the composition. Each raga would indicate a mood such as "dawn", "beauty" or "spring". Of equal importance as the theme (*raga*), was the rhythm pattern (*tala*) of the music. Ragas were classified according to the time of night or day that was appropriate for their performance.

The Indians used many instruments to play their music.

Musical Instruments

Mridanga	A barrel shaped drum with both ends covered with parchment.
Tambura	A lute, the pitch of which could be changed.
Vina	This instrument had strings stretched over a plate with a parchment covered drum at one end and a gourd at the other.
Venu	A bamboo flute.
Nagasvaram	A long oboe-like instrument with a double reed.
Kañjirá	Tambourine.
Sitār	Long necked lute.
Gongs	There were various gongs.

The singing voice was also regarded as a musical instrument.

Dancing

Indian dancing has changed little over the centuries and modern dancers still dance to certain traditional rules. Dancing (nrtya) was closely connected to acting (nātya), and these are both forms of the same word. Indian dancing was done with the whole body and every movement, expression and gesture was significant and carefully controlled and co-ordinated.

There were many folk dances performed at ancient Indian festivals but in later times dancing in public was permitted only by professional dancers.

Shiva was the god of dance and it was believed that his dancing symbolised the movement of the world. All temples had their dancers or *devadasis* whose dances represented the rhythms and nature of the universe.

Dance Dramas

The royal courts and temples were the original places where dramas, dancers and musicians performed. In the very early times entertainers were not highly regarded but this had changed by the 8th century.

Ancient Hindu Theatre

Productions were held in small theatres as the drama depended upon gestures, some of which were quite subtle such as eye movement which could only be performed before small audiences. Sanskrit dramas prohibited any death or defeat of the hero. Hindu theatre was of two types: *Lokadharmî* which was realistic theatre showing human behaviour, and *nátyadharmî*, a more stylised drama using mostly gestures and symbols.

Above: 18th century painting of a dance performance attended by Maharana Raj Singh III. The female musician to the left of the dancers is playing a sitar, and the musician on the right in the foreground is playing a classical drone lute.

During the days of the Mauryan Empire, court entertainers consisted of troupes of acrobats, magicians, snake charmers, wrestlers and dancers accompanied by musicians.

Other Recreations

Dice games were popular with some of the earliest dice being found in India. The earliest dates back to 3000 B.C. while by 1400 B.C. the dice closer resembled the dice as we know it. Dice is mentioned in the *Mahābhārata* and Vedic hymns. Board games were popular including a game called *shaturanga* which was a forerunner to modern chess. Religious festivals and feats including the Hindu festival of *Holī* (which is still held in March each year) included many different rituals which were regarded as entertainment as well as having religious significance.

35

Wars and Battles

The Aryans showed a liking for wars and conquests. The first Aryans were divided into three classes: nobles who chose one of their own as chief or **raja**; priests who were responsible for religious teaching and observation, and tribesmen who were the herders of cattle.

As the Aryans moved south, they conquered the lands and the people. They defended their newly conquered lands from outside attacks with armies recruited from the old noble class of warriors.

During the period between the Mauryan and Gupta empires, India was invaded again by many people including those from the countries of Persia, Afghanistan and Central Asia. The first invaders in the 4th century B.C. were the Greeks under Alexander the Great. Invasions in early times were all confined to the north.

In the south-west the warrior **Rajput maharajahs**, thought to be descended from central Asian tribes, lived. They divided the land into petty kingdoms and ruled much of northern India. These people were accepted by the Hindus as members of the Hindu warrior class. They had a passion for war and constantly waged attacks upon each other. They only united at the time of the Muslim invasions in an attempt to defend the Hindu way of life but were eventually defeated by the Muslims.

Battle Dress

Quilted coats, turbans and trousers was standard protective battle dress in northern India until the 19th century. Shields of cane covered with leather were also used.

There were many types of Indian soldiers, including ordinary troops, mercenaries, deserters from the enemy and tribesmen used as guerillas. The warrior class were the ksatriya but all classes took part in war, and in early

Detail of a painting depicting a cavalry battle in the 13th century.

times all free men were required to perform military service although they were not conscripted.

The Indian army had four divisions: elephants, cavalry, chariots and infantry. The basic unit of the Indian army was the *patti*, consisting of one elephant, one chariot, three horses and five foot soldiers.

Elephants

The Buddhist scriptures first mention elephants being trained for war, and King Bimbisara of Magadha owned a large and efficient elephant corps. The elephants acted like tanks in a modern army, by smashing gates, walls and other defences and a line of elephants provided a bridge across shallow streams.

Elephants often wore leather armour and had their tusks tipped with metal spikes. Elephants went into battle with a **mahout** and two or three soldiers who were armed with bows, javelins and long spears. The fighting elephants struck terror into the hearts of an enemy, but they were able to be defeated in battle in spite of their psychological advantage and sheer strength. Elephants were easily frightened by fire and were apt to throw their riders and trample the fallen troops as they trumpeted and stampeded in panic.

Cavalry

The cavalry consisted of bands of foot soldiers, and were the weakest section of the Indian army. They were easily defeated by mounted archers.

Chariots

These were popular in early Vedic times and right up to the Christian era. Early sculpture shows fighting chariots. The chariot of early

times was light and pulled by two horses and carried a driver and a warrior. There were four horse chariots which carried four men.

Infantry

The infantry made up the majority of the Indian army. Some early accounts give some idea of the size of the army. The last Nanda king was supposed to have commanded 20,000 cavalry, 2,000 chariots, 200,000 infantry and 3,000 to 6,000 elephants. Harasa had 60,000 elephants and 100,000 cavalry. (The medieval armies were larger than those of earlier periods.)

Painting from the Mogul dynasty showing Akbar's attack against a Rajput fortress in 1568. This picture shows the battle dress and weapons of the period. In the background, the warriors are carrying guns.

Weapons

Weapons consisted of **ballistas, battering rams** and an Indian bow which in Mauryan times was up to 2 metres (7 feet) long, made of bamboo and fired cane arrows. Poisoned arrows were also used. There were various types of swords including a long two-handed slashing sword called a *nistrimsa*. There were also lances including the *tomara*. The long lance was used in fighting while mounted on the back of an elephant. Iron maces and battle axes were also used.

Forts

The building and use of forts was a very important part of defences in early India but nearly all forts were adapted and rebuilt after the Muslim era. A fortified city was called a *durga*, and fortifications consisted of an earthwork planted with thorny shrubs with a high wall. Built into the walls were square towers and balconies for archers.

The most important pre-Muslim fortress is Devagiri (now modern Daulatābād) although the outer fortifications were replaced and adapted by the Muslims.

The Indian army resembled a gigantic city on the move. Not only was the army itself large, but followers including wives and families of members of the army, moved with it. An Indian army camp was not an organised disciplined military camp.

Rites of Battle

Battle was regarded as a religious rite and many rituals preceeded it. The day and time of battle was often decided by astrologers and purification rites were carefully observed the eve before the battle.

The general organisation of a battle and deployment of forces was: heavy infantry at the centre, light infantry, chariots and cavalry on the wings, elephants in the centre and archers behind the spearmen. In legends, great emphasis was placed on combats between single warriors, but battles were usually won by mass fighting.

Prisoners of war were rarely put to death. They were mostly released on payment of a ransom. The very poor, were usually enslaved and paid their own ransom by way of labour.

The building and use of forts such as this one, the Jaiselmer Fortress, were an important part of Indian defense. The Jaiselmer Castle was built in the 12th century, and is situated close to the West Pakistan border.

Indian Inventions and Special Skills

Use of Elephants

Indians used elephants in work and war. Tame elephants were certainly used at the time of Buddha. As elephants rarely bred in captivity they had to be captured live and tamed. Large areas of forest were declared elephant reserves and professional trackers, hunters and tamers were employed. Generally only kings and chiefs could afford to own elephants.

The use of war elephants was greatly depended upon by Indian fighting forces and they were used to great effect to terrorise the enemy and to break down enemy embattlements.

Hinduism

The Hindus developed a **philosophy** which involved an inquiry into the nature of knowledge and the limit of reason which was quite different from the philosophy of the West and greatly influenced it. It was from this whole view of life and knowledge that Hinduism evolved. The word Hinduism means "the civilisation of the Hindus", which gradually developed from the ancient civilisation. In principle, Hinduism can absorb all kinds of belief and does not depend on the existence of god or whether god is one or many.

Iron Casting

The art of casting iron was developed in India long before it was known in Europe. Some Indian iron pillars are still standing untarnished and unrusted today after fifteen centuries. Iron was smelted in small coal burning furnaces.

The Iron Pillar of Meharauli near Delhi is evidence of Indian expertise. This pillar made from a single piece of iron is over 6 metres

Elephants, which have roamed the Indian landscape for thousands of years, were put to many uses by the Indians. This 18th century painting shows elephants being herded for the Maharana Sangram Singh.

(20 feet) high. It is thought to have been a memorial to King Candra Gupta II. This pillar has not rusted even though it has been exposed to over fifteen hundred monsoons.

Medical Knowledge and Skill

Indians have had a thorough and advanced knowledge of medicine since ancient times. They used many medicinal plants, and knew of many surgical techniques. Although they did not have antiseptics they understood the value of fresh air and light in curing sickness. Narcotics were often used as forms of anaesthetic. It has been debated by historians as to whether the Greeks gained any of their medical knowledge from the Indians. However, the Indians had little idea of the function of the brain and thought the heart was the seat of intelligence.

Growing of Cotton

Cotton growing appeared earlier in India than elsewhere. The Greek historian Herodotus wrote of "the trees growing wool instead of fruit", from which the Indians made fabrics for clothing. The Arabs learned of this from India and their word *"quattan"* eventually found its way into the English language as "cotton".

Mathematical Knowledge

The Indians evolved a system of mathematics which was superior to that of the Greeks (except for geometry). They also invented a decimal system and Arabic numerals both of which reached the West via the Arabs.

The Gypsies

For many years it was thought that the European gypsies came originally from Egypt but it is now though that from 1763 onwards the gypsies had Indian origins. A study of the gypsy language, Romani, shows it to be an

18th century miniature painting depicting women playing chess. It is believed by archaeologists that chess originated in India.

Indo-Aryan language and it is now recognised that gypsies probably had Indian origins. The culture of the colourful gypsies with their special dancing and music has been called one of India's gifts to the world.

Familiar Legends and Tales

It would seem that many of the world's "fairy-tales" had their origins in India, being collected first in the *Panchatantra* and then in the *Hitopadesha*. These tales found their way via the Arabs to the Western world. Many became merged with Arabian tales such as the *A Thousand and One Nights* and others inspired La Fontaine and Hans Christian Andersen.

Chess

It has been accepted by archaeologists that chess originated in India. In its original form it had four players and used a dice to determine the moves. The game was played as four campaigning armies and the pieces were a king, an elephant, a horse, a chariot or ship, and four footmen. This game was also taken from India by the Arabs to the Western world.

Why the Civilisation Declined

By A.D. 1200 India and its civilisation had totally changed. By this time Buddhism was not as important, and the great University at Nalanda had been destroyed. Hinduism was the main religion, the Brahmans were powerful and many Indian customs had changed. The Muslim conquest beginning in A.D. 1193 and lasting until 1757 had the most impact on the physical appearance of India. To the rest of the world the Muslim Empire (the Rajputs) in India appeared as a unified whole but this was not so. Hindu chiefs still ruled many parts of India but had to pay tribute to their Muslim overlords.

The Muslims destroyed the old temples and palaces as they conquered parts of India and eventually left in their place many mosques, tombs and Muslim palaces. (The Hindus did not build tombs.) Because there were so many Muslim structures these gave the outward appearance that these people had dominated the culture. In the south of India the Muslims had little influence. Although many people were converted to the Muslim faith, there were only a few regions where the majority of Indians were persuaded to do so.

Hindu and Muslim lived side by side for centuries, and borrowed from each other's culture. There were some areas and periods of persecution of Hindus but this was not sustained.

Eventually the Muslim power broke down, and the Europeans including the Portuguese, Dutch, Danes, French and British, found their way to India. By the 19th century the British had colonised the Indian subcontinent.

However, from the time of the Muslims, Indian society withdrew into itself and became a very conservative society which preferred links with the past to links with a changing world. It was other cultures and societies beginning with the Muslims who made changes over the face of India and intruded into Indian civilisation. But the civilisation did not really disappear, for in the late 19th century, the Hindu culture began to reassert itself.

People bathing in the sacred Ganges River, as they have for thousands of years.

Glossary

Alluvial soil   Deposits of sand and mud which are brought downstream by rivers and deposited on the lowlands. It provides fertile soil for crops.

Archaeological records   The remains of a civilisation which have been discovered by careful digging around a site. The items are then described and recorded.

Bodhisattvas   Buddhas who renounced their right to Nirvana and came back to earth to help others become enlightened.

Caste   The system by which Hindu society was organised. One was born into a certain caste and this remained unchanged throughout one's life. Each caste was allocated specific duties, obligations, occupations and rights. Castes in Hindu society were: Brahmans (priests); Kshatriyas (fighters and warriors); Vaisyas (merchants); Shudras (working people); and Outcasts or Pariahs (slaves, and captives of war).

Civet Cat   Meat eating cat-like mammal of southern Asia.

Cobra   Best known of the Indian reptiles. There were two varieties of cobra, the king cobra and the common cobra both of which grow up to 3 to 4 metres (15 feet) long.

Concubines   Secondary wives who live with their partner without being married to him.

Cremation   The practice of burning a corpse to ashes, instead of burying it in a coffin in the ground.

Deciduous   Trees which lose their leaves once each year, usually during the coldest months.

Dharma   The rule of life as determined by one's caste. To the Hindus, to accept one's place in the caste system was to automatically accept the limitations, rights and obligations that went with this.

Dhoti   A loin cloth traditionally worn in India by Hindu men. It was wrapped around the hips and thighs with one end brought between the legs and tucked into the waistband. When in place the dhoti resembled baggy knee-length trousers.

Evergreen   Trees and shrubs which do not lose their leaves at any time during the year.

Glacier   A river of ice which moves slowly. As it moves it cuts through the earth. When glaciers melt they leave very distinctive V-shaped valleys.

Gopuram   An elaborate gateway or gate-tower to a Hindu temple.

Hypnosis   An induced sleeplike state during which people experience visions of past experiences. Hypnosis is used as a medical cure in some cases.

Ibex   A wild goat with large recurved horns.

Incantation   A chanting or uttering of words and prayers supposed to have religious or magical power.

Karma   A Buddhist belief adopted by the Hindus where a person's conduct in one life is rewarded or punished in future lives. During the course of a chain of lives, individuals can perfect themselves.

Khaddar   A garment of coarse hand-spun or hand-woven cloth, worn by Indian women.

Krait   A deadly venomous snake. Eleven species of Kraits are found in India.

Lac   Resinous substance deposited on twigs of various trees by the lac insect and used as a red colouring.

Lampblack   A fine black pigment consisting of almost pure carbon collected as soot from the smoke of burning oil and gas.

Lentils   A plant whose flat seeds have a food value similar to peas and beans. Lentils are used in soups or they can be soaked, and mixed with flour and other vegetables, and fried.

Litter   A portable bed or couch which could be opened or closed, and mounted on two poles and carried at each end on men's shoulders or by animals.

Mahout   The keeper and driver of an elephant.

Maharajah   Great king; a title given to certain great ruling princes of India.

Mangrove A tree found in subtropical and tropical countries which grows on salt and mud flats.

Markhor A kind of wild goat with spiral horns and long shaggy hair.

Monsoon A seasonal wind which blows across the Indian Ocean toward India bringing heavy rainfall. Crops planted by Indian peasants depended upon the monsoon rains. If these failed to arrive or were late, crops failed and people starved.

Nomadic Moving from place to place with no fixed place of living. The early Aryans moved from place to place seeking pasture for their herds.

Oral transmission Passed on by word of mouth as opposed to being written down. People unable to read or write pass on information, legends, songs, and customs in this way, from generation to generation.

Ordeal A severe test or trial; primitive form of trial used to determine guilt or innocence, by the effect of fire, poison or water upon the accused. The result was regarded as a divine judgement.

Philosophy A study which attempts to discover underlying truths about all knowledge and reality.

Pyre A pile or heap of wood or other material which can burn. Funeral pyres were lit to burn a corpse to ashes. This was a Hindu custom. In early times it was decreed that widows should also be cremated on their husbands' funeral pyre.

Raja A king or prince. (A great king was called a maharaja).

Rajputs People half-native and half-descended from invading Scythians and Huns who built a feudal civilisation ruled by warlike rajas. They helped defend Hinduism from the Muslim invaders but were eventually overpowered.

Reincarnation A belief shared by Hindus and Buddhists that the soul, upon death of the body, moves to another body or form.

Sal A tree with a close grained hard wood.

Sanskrit Ancient classical literary language of India, introduced by the Aryans.

Sari An outer garment worn by Indian women. It consisted of a brightly coloured or embroidered silk or cotton fabric, several metres (yards) long. It was worn wrapped around the body with one end left hanging or used to cover the head.

Soma A milky fermented liquor produced from the soma plant and used in Vedic sacrifices.

Stupa A Buddhist commemorative monument usually housing sacred relics associated with Buddha, or an architectural symbol of Buddha's death.

Sutra Concise rules or teachings in Buddhist and Hindu literature.

Suttee An Indian custom whereby a widow burned herself either on the funeral pyre of her dead husband or soon after his death. Memorials to women who died in this way are found throughout India. It was a common practice in India at the time of Alexander the Great's visit there. One Punjab tribe made suttee a law to prevent wives from poisoning their husbands.

Tamarind Fruit of a large tropical tree; also the tree cultivated for its fruit.

Vedas Books of Hindu sacred knowledge. They contain sacred hymns and verses composed in Sanskrit.

Vegetarian One who eats vegetable food only, and believes that this constitutes the only proper diet for people.

Viper A deadly venomous snake. Twenty species are found in India.

Yak Wild long-haired ox.

Yogis Holy Men who, after special training through eight separate stages, learnt how to separate body and mind, and could consequently perform many feats which they believed were purifying. The feats, such as walking on hot coals, are performed without feeling pain.

Some Famous People and Places

Chandra Gupta I

Chandra Gupta was founder of the imperial dynasty of the Guptas and ruled India from A.D. 320 to about 330. Much about his early life is unknown but he became a local chief in the kingdom of Magadha and increased his power by marrying Princess Kumāradevi whose people (the Licchavi) controlled the northern lands. It is thought that the year A.D. 320 (used as the date of the commencement of the Gupta era) was either the date of his marriage or coronation. By the end of his reign he was claiming the title Mahārāja-dhirāja, "king of kings".

His son, Samudra Gupta conquered more lands and eventually the Gupta Empire was founded.

Chandra Gupta II (also known as Vikramāditya)

Chandra Gupta was in fact the third of the Guptas and son of Samudra Gupta. He governed a very extensive empire. Some of the silver coins of his reign are inscribed Vikramāditya, meaning the "Son of Valour". His capital was at Pātaliputra (now called Patna). Under his reign India enjoyed peace and prosperity and during this time, too, arts and learning flourished. He established free rest-houses and hospitals, and dispensed medicines and other commodities to the needy. Chandra Gupta II was a Hindu but also tolerated the practise of the Buddhist and Jain religion.

Chandragupta Maurya

Chandragupta Maurya was founder of the Mauryan dynasty and reigned from about 322 to 298 B.C. He was the first emperor to unify India under one administration.

He was born of poor parents and his father died while he was quite young, leaving the family destitute. His uncles gave him to a cowherd who brought him up as their own son. Later he was sold to a hunter to look after cattle. His was purchased again by a Brahman politician named Cānakya and taken to Taxila (modern Pakistan) where he was educated and taught military tactics. It was here that he met Alexander the Great.

On Cānakya's advice, he raised an army and defeated the forces of the Nanda dynasty. He became king of the Magadha kingdom and ruler of the Punjab and began the Maurya dynasty. He expanded the borders of his empire still further until it reached from the Himalayas and modern Afghanistan to the southern tip of India. This was one of the largest empires in the history of the world.

During a twelve year famine, in which he could do nothing to relieve their suffering, he fasted to death in sorrow for his people.

Faxian

Faxian was a Chinese Buddhist monk who lived in the 4th century A.D. He journeyed to India in 402 to visit the sites of Buddha's life and to take back to China any previously unknown Buddhist texts. He studied such texts in Indian for ten years and finally took many copies of texts back to China where he translated them from Sanskrit into Chinese.

The record of his journeys in China was written in the *Fu Kuo Chi* (*Record of Buddhist Kingdoms*). This is a detailed record of his extensive travels in China in which he reported on everything he saw, including the temperature of the winds, the variety of animal and bird life, descriptions of mountains and rivers as well as the people.

On his return trip to China, his ship was driven ashore in a violent storm. From here (thought to have been Java) he took another ship, only to be driven off course by another storm and forced to spend 200 days at sea. He finally reached China.

The Ganges

The Ganges is the greatest river of northern India and sacred to the Hindus. It rises in the Himalayas and flows through the plains for 2,506 kilometres (1,557 miles) before it reaches the sea.

According to the legends, this river originally flowed in heaven but was brought to earth by the King of Bhagīratha to purify the ashes of his ancestors. The river (personified as a goddess) reluctantly did as she was asked. She fell to earth, cascading onto the head of Shiva so as to break her fall. The spirit of the Ganges is believed by many to be one of the wives of Shiva.

Pilgrims come regularly to bathe in the Ganges.

The Himalayas

This great system of mountains includes the highest mountains in the world. There are more than thirty peaks with the highest, Mt Everest rising to 8,848 metres (29,000 feet). Because of their great height, the Himalayas are permanently snow-capped.

The name is derived from the Sanskrit *hima*, meaning "snow" and *ālava*, meaning "abode". These mountains provided an impassable barrier between the northern lands of India and the areas to the north.

Ashoka

Ashoka was the last major emperor of the Mauryan dynasty of India, ruling from about 265 to 238 B.C. He was deeply distressed by the terrible suffering inflicted on his people during wars. He was also influenced by the Buddhist faith and was impressed by its nature of peace. He vowed to live by the principle of *dharma*, or the right life, and was determined to lead a non-agressive life.

He made announcements to people and had messages engraved on rocks and pillars. (These were later called Rock Edicts and Pillar Edicts). He also ordered his officials to preach the dharma to people and even founded a special class of "dharma ministers" to do this work.

He ordered all matters concerning public welfare to be reported to him. He also founded hospitals for people and animals, made medicines readily available, planted trees along roadsides, had wells sunk and watering sheds and rest-houses built. He made cruelty to animals a major offence.

He built many stupas and monasteries in the service of Buddhism and aided Buddhist missionaries.

Buddha

Buddha, whose real name was Siddhārtha Gautama and who was known as the 'Enlightened (or Awakened) One' was the founder of the Buddhist religion.

According to the traditional legend, he was born of the kshatriyas or warrior caste in about 563 B.C. There are many stories about his youth. He was supposed to have been married at 16 to his cousin Yasodharā who was also 16 years old, and he lived a very comfortable life. By the age of 29 he became concerned about the suffering in the world. He gave up his comfortable way of life, left his wife and son and went in search of people who could teach him the truth about life. Although he was unable to find a teacher who could teach him all he wanted to know, he is supposed to have become enlightened while sitting under a banyan tree at a place now known as Buddh Gayā or Bodh Gayā. For the rest of his life he taught his followers and others the dharma.

At the age of 80, Buddha and a group of followers set out on a journey north. He died at Kusinārā (modern Kasia) in about 483 B.C. Ashoka erected a pillar at Buddha's birth place, now called Rummindei in present day Nepal.

Index

Acknowledgements

The author and publishers are grateful to the following for permission to reproduce copyright photographs and prints:

Australasian Nature Transparencies: (S. Hodgkiss) pp.11, 38, (NHPA) pp.12, 13, 31, (Tony Howard) p.14, (John O'Neil) p.23, (Silvestris) p.41; BBC Hulton Picture Library pp.10, 26; Ronald Sheridan/The Ancient Art and Architecture Collection pp.15, 20, 21, 22, 30, 32, 33, 35, 39; Werner Forman Archive: cover, pp.18, 27, 28, 29, 40.

While every care has been taken to trace and acknowledge copyright, the publishers tender their apologies for any accidental infringement where copyright has proved untraceable. They would be pleased to come to a suitable arrangement with the rightful owner in each case.

Cover design, maps and art: Stephen Pascoe

First published 1989 by
THE MACMILLAN COMPANY OF AUSTRALIA PTY LTD
107 Moray Street, South Melbourne 3205
6 Clarke Street, Crows Nest 2065

Associated companies and representatives
throughout the world.

National Library of Australia
cataloguing in publication data.

Odijk, Pamela, 1942–
  The Indians.

  Includes index.
  ISBN 0 333 47781 2.

  1. India — Social life and customs — To 1200
  — Juvenile literature. I. Title. (Series :
  Odijk, Pamela, 1942–   Ancient world).

934

Set in Optima by Setrite Typesetters, Hong Kong
Printed in Hong Kong

Oceania | Europe | Africa

Australian Aborigines	**Maori**	**Melanesians**	**Greeks**	**Romans**	**Angles, Saxons & Jutes**	**Britons**	**Vikings**	**Egyptians**	**First Africans**

Oceania — c50 000 B.C. Aborigines inhabit continent

Africa — 40 000 Evolution of man

Year	Australian Aborigines	Maori	Melanesians	Greeks	Romans	Angles, Saxons & Jutes	Britons	Vikings	Egyptians	First Africans
8000	Torres and Bass Straits under water							The Baltic — freshwater lake		Farm settlements
7500										
7000	Lake Nitchie settled			Neolithic Age / Settled agriculture						
6500										
6000										
5500										
5000	South Australian settlements								Egypt-early farms	Increased trade across Sahara
4500										
4000							Hunting and gathering			
3500	Ord Valley settlement								Predynastic	
3000				Bronze Age				The first farmers		
2500				Crete — palaces / Mainland building					Old Kingdom / Giza pyramids	
2000							Megalithic monuments raised		Middle Kingdom	Sahara become desert
1500								Bronze Age	New Kingdom	
1000				Dark Age			Farms and buildings established	New Kingdom declines		Kushites
500 B.C.				Colonisation / City-states established / Classical Age / Wars — lands extended	Rome found / Republic established / Rome expands through Italy and foreign lands		Ogham alphabet in use	Celtic Iron Age / Roman Iron Age	Persian conquest / Greek conquest / Roman rule	Nok / Greek influence
0 B.C./A.D.		Legend: Kupe found New Zealand and told people how to reach there		Hellenistic Age / Empire divided, lands lost. / Culture enters new phase	Empire begins: Augustus — emperor / End of Western Roman Empire	Hengist and Horsa arrived in Kent / England: 12 kingdoms	Roman invasion / Britain becomes two provinces / Saxons settle	Vendel period		Kushites' power ends
500 A.D.						Athelstan rules all England / Norman Conquest		Army invade England / Christianity adopted / Viking laws recorded		Arabs settle east coast / Christian European slave trade
1000	Dutch explorers sight Aborigines / First White settlers	Maori arrive / Great Britain annexed New Zealand	Europeans dominate / Cook's voyages / Christianity is introduced							Europeans divide Africa
1500										
2000										